Olympic Greats

OLYMPIC COMBAT SPORT LEGENDS

MARTIN GITLIN

BLACK
RABBIT
BOOKS

Bolt is published by Black Rabbit Books
P.O. Box 3263, Mankato, Minnesota, 56002.
www.blackrabbitbooks.com
Copyright © 2021 Black Rabbit Books

Jen Besel, editor; Catherine Cates, designer;
Omay Ayres, photo researcher

All rights reserved. No part of this book may be reproduced,
stored in a retrieval system or transmitted in any form or by any means, electronic,
mechanical, photocopying, recording, or otherwise, without written permission
from the publisher.

Library of Congress Cataloging-in-Publication Data
Names: Gitlin, Marty, author.
Title: Olympic combat sports legends / by Martin Gitlin.
Other titles: Combat sports legends | Bolt (North Mankato, Minn.)
Description: Mankato, Minnesota : Bolt is published by Black Rabbit Books, 2021.
| Series: Bolt. Olympic greats | Includes webography. | Includes bibliographic
references and index. | Audience: Ages 8-12 years |
Audience: Grades 4-6 Identifiers: LCCN 2019028400 (print) | ISBN 9781623102654
(Hardcover) | ISBN 9781644663615 (Paperback) | ISBN 9781623103590 (eBook)
Subjects: LCSH: Hand-to-hand fighting—Records. | Mixed martial arts—Records. |
Olympic athletes—Juvenile literature. | Olympics—History—Juvenile literature.
Classification: LCC GV1111 .G52 2021 (print) | LCC GV1111 (ebook) |
DDC 796.8—dc23
LC record available at https://lccn.loc.gov/2019028400
LC ebook record available at https://lccn.loc.gov/2019028401

Printed in the United States. 2/20

All statistics are through the 2016 Olympic Games.

Image Credits

CONTENTS

CHAPTER 1

Amazing

ATHLETES

They kick, punch, and flip. Some even fight with swords. Athletes in **combat sports** have to be tough. The world's best compete in the Summer Olympics.

The Summer Games are held every four years. Countries send their best athletes to compete.

OLYMPIC COMBAT SPORTS

The Summer Olympics has six combat sports.

BOXING

fighting
with fists

FENCING

fighting
with swords

JUDO

a martial art
where
athletes fight
using quick
movements

GRECO-ROMAN WRESTLING

wrestling in which the arms and upper body are used to bring down an opponent

TAE KWON DO

a martial art featuring kicks and punches

FREESTYLE WRESTLING

wrestling in which the whole body is used to bring down an opponent

COUNTRY
HUNGARY

1932, 1936,
1948, 1952, 1956, 1960
OLYMPIC YEARS

BRONZE
MEDALS
2

1
SILVER
MEDALS

GOLD
MEDALS
7

CHAPTER 2

Powerful

PLAYERS

• • • • • Aladar Gerevich
Fencing

Many people call Aladar Gerevich the greatest fencer ever. He helped win six straight team golds in one event. That's an Olympic record.

Gerevich won 10 medals. He might have won more. But the Olympics weren't held during World War II. He couldn't go in 1940 and 1944.

Kayla Harrison
Judo

In 2012, Kayla Harrison won gold in judo. She was the first American to win that sport. Then she did it again in 2016. She fought eight Olympic matches. And she won them all.

COUNTRY **UNITED STATES**

OLYMPIC YEARS 2012, 2016

BRONZE MEDALS 0 SILVER MEDALS 0 GOLD MEDALS 2

Karelin almost won a fourth gold in 2000.
But Rulon Gardner beat him in the finals. Some say
it's the biggest **upset** in the sport's history.

Aleksandr Karelin
Greco-Roman Wrestling

Aleksandr Karelin was a powerful Greco-Roman wrestler. Some think he's the best ever. He used his incredible strength to take down opponents. He won 19 straight Olympic matches.

The Soviet Union no longer exists. It broke into several nations in 1991.

COUNTRY SOVIET UNION AND RUSSIA

OLYMPIC YEARS 1988, 1992, 1996, 2000

BRONZE MEDALS 0 **SILVER MEDALS** 1 **GOLD MEDALS** 3

Pal Kovacs
Fencing

Pal Kovacs went to five Olympics. He helped win the team sabre event every time. He also medaled twice in the individual. In 1952, he was on fire. He won all his matches.

COUNTRY **HUNGARY**

OLYMPIC YEARS 1936, 1948, 1952, 1956, 1960

BRONZE MEDALS **1**   SILVER MEDALS **0**   GOLD MEDALS **6**

Fencing Events

Olympic fencers can compete in three events. Medals are awarded for individual and team fencing.

FOIL

uses a light blade to poke opponents' upper bodies

EPEE

uses a heavier blade to poke opponents from head to toe

SABRE

uses a short blade to slash toward opponents' upper bodies

Hwang Kyung-seon
Tae Kwon Do

Hwang Kyung-seon had great speed. She often kicked opponents' heads. She won three individual tae kwon do medals. She's the first woman to do that. Kyung-seon lost one match in 2004. She never lost another one.

COUNTRY
SOUTH KOREA

2004, 2008, 2012
OLYMPIC YEARS

BRONZE MEDALS
1

GOLD MEDALS
2

0
SILVER MEDALS

TIMELINE

The modern Olympics started in 1896. Female combat athletes could not compete for many years. Here's when women's events started.

FENCING
1924

JUDO
1992

2000

TAE KWON DO

2012

BOXING

2004

FREESTYLE WRESTLING

THERE ARE CURRENTLY NO WOMEN'S EVENTS IN GRECO-ROMAN WRESTLING.

Aleksandr Medved

Freestyle Wrestling

Aleksandr Medved was a powerful athlete. He often won against heavier wrestlers. In 1972, he weighed about 225 pounds (102 kilograms). He took down an opponent who weighed more than 400 pounds (181 kg). Many believe Medved was the best freestyle wrestler ever. In three Olympics, no one beat him.

COUNTRY **SOVIET UNION**

OLYMPIC YEARS 1964, 1968, 1972

BRONZE MEDALS | SILVER MEDALS | GOLD MEDALS

0 | 0 | 3

MOST OLYMPIC WRESTLING MEDALS
(Men's and Women's Freestyle and Greco-Roman combined)

	MEDALS
BULGARIA	69
JAPAN	69
FINLAND	83
SWEDEN	86
SOVIET UNION	116
UNITED STATES	132

MEDALS 0   30   60   90   120   150

Tadahiro Nomura
Judo

Tadahiro Nomura is the first three-time Olympic judo champion. He is known for a move called "drop seoi nage." He would drop to his knees. At the same time, he'd roll his opponent over his back. The person would fall onto the mat.

COUNTRY	JAPAN	
OLYMPIC YEARS	1996, 2000, 2004	
BRONZE MEDALS	SILVER MEDALS	GOLD MEDALS
0	0	3

Nomura

Hadi Saei
Tae Kwon Do

Hadi Saei has three Olympic medals. He won gold at two different weight classes. He won the **featherweight** division in 2004. He then gained weight. He won at **welterweight** four years later.

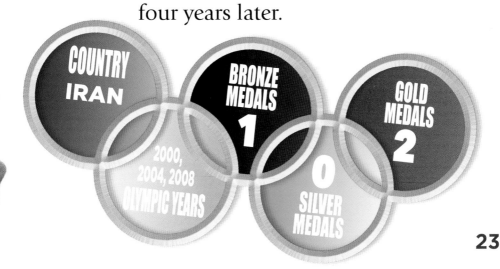

COUNTRY
IRAN

2000, 2004, 2008
OLYMPIC YEARS

BRONZE MEDALS
1

0
SILVER MEDALS

GOLD MEDALS
2

Teofilo Stevenson
Boxing

Teofilo Stevenson was a tough boxer. He used his powerful right hand to win. He often won matches with a single-punch **knockout**. Opponents knew the punch was coming. But they couldn't stop it.

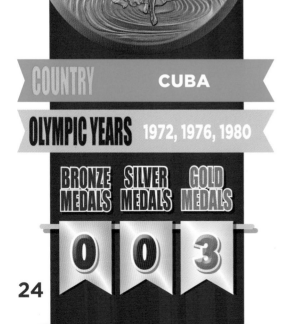

COUNTRY	CUBA	

OLYMPIC YEARS	1972, 1976, 1980	

BRONZE MEDALS	SILVER MEDALS	GOLD MEDALS
0	0	3

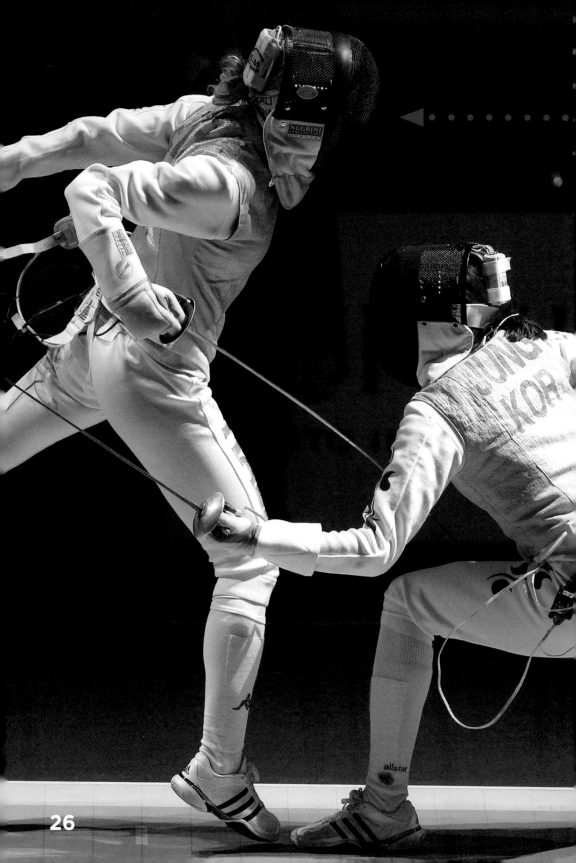

Valentina Vezzali
Fencing

No female fencer has more Olympic golds than Valentina Vezzali. She earned three individual gold medals. She also helped the Italian team take three more. She competed in 62 Olympic matches. She only lost seven times.

COUNTRY
ITALY

BRONZE MEDALS
2

GOLD MEDALS
6

1996, 2000, 2004, 2008, 2012
OLYMPIC YEARS

1
SILVER MEDALS

CHAPTER 3

Comparing

Combat sport athletes push to be the greatest during the Olympics. Compare the stats of some of the best.

TOTAL MEDALS

NUMBER OF MEDALS

10 — 10
8 — 9
6 — 7
4 — 4
2 — 3
0

Aladar Gerevich
Valentina Vezzali
Pal Kovacs
Aleksandr Karelin
Hwang Kyung-seon

OLYMPIC APPEARANCES

Name	Number of Olympic Appearances
Kayla Harrison	2
Hwang Kyung-seon	3
Aleksandr Medved	3
Tadahiro Nomura	3
Hadi Saei	3
Teofilo Stevenson	3
Aleksandr Karelin	4
Pal Kovacs	5
Valentina Vezzali	5
Aladar Gerevich	6

NUMBER OF OLYMPIC APPEARANCES

0 1 2 3 4 5 6

3
Aleksandr Medved

3
Tadahiro Nomura

3
Hadi Saei

3
Teofilo Stevenson

2
Kayla Harrison

combat sport (KOHM-bat SPOHRT)—a competitive fighting activity usually between two athletes

featherweight (FEH-thur-WAYT)—a weight category in which athletes of a similar size compete; in men's Olympic tae kwon do, it's 129 to 150 pounds (58 to 68 kg); for women it's 108 to 126 pounds (49 to 57 kg).

knockout (NOK-ouwt)—the end of a boxing match when one boxer has been knocked down and is unable to get up and keep boxing within a certain time

martial art (MAR-shul ART)—any of several arts of combat and self-defense (such as judo or tae kwon do) that are widely practiced as a sport

opponent (uh-POH-nunt)—a person, team, or group that is competing against another

upset (UP-set)—an unexpected defeat

welterweight (WEL-tur-WAYT)—a weight category in which athletes of a similar size compete; in men's Olympic tae kwon do, it's 150 to 176 pounds (68 to 80 kg); for women it's 126 to 148 pounds (57 to 67 kg).

BOOKS

Hellebuyck, Adam, and Laura Deimel. *Olympics.* Global Citizens: Sports. Ann Arbor, MI: Cherry Lake Publishing, 2019.

Osborne, M. K. *Combat Sports.* Summer Olympic Sports. Mankato, MN: Amicus, 2020.

Sherman, Jill. *Wrestling.* Let's Play Sports! Minneapolis: Bellwether Media, Inc., 2020.

WEBSITES

Olympics Coverage from SI Kids
www.sikids.com/olympics

Quick Guide to Olympic Fencing
www.youtube.com/watch?v=69VJIjKX_lE

Sports | List of Summer and Winter Olympic Sports
www.olympic.org/sports

INDEX